Maryland Landscapes of Eugene Leake

CRAIG HANKIN

MARYLAND LANDSCAPES OF

THE JOHNS HOPKINS UNIVERSITY PRESS   BALTIMORE & LONDON

The Johns Hopkins University Press,
701 West 40th Street,
Baltimore, Maryland 21211
The Johns Hopkins Press Ltd., London

The paper used in this publication meets the minimum requirements
of American National Standard for Information Sciences—Perma-
nence of Paper for Printed Library Materials, ANSI Z39.48-1984
∞ ™

Library of Congress Cataloging-in-Publication Data

Hankin, Craig.
    Maryland landscapes of Eugene Leake.

    1. Leake, Eugene, 1911–   —Catalogs. 2. Maryland in art—
Catalogs. 3. Leake, Eugene, 1911–   . 4. Landscape painters—
Maryland—Biography. I. Leake, Eugene, 1911–   . II. Title.
ND237.L43A4   1986   759.13   [B]   86-45437
ISBN 0-8018-3366-3 (alk. paper)

To the memory of my grandfather, Charles S. Bernstein

Acknowledgments

There are a number of people whom I would like to thank for making my work easier.

At the Maryland Institute of Art, Abby Sangiamo, Grace Hartigan, and Norman Carlberg were most generous with their time and memories. So was John Stoneham, who in addition gave me access to his extensive files. Raoul Middleman deserves mention here, too, as does W. Bowdoin Davis, Jr., a person with as keen an appreciation of my subject as anyone.

At the Johns Hopkins University, I received invaluable support from Chris Colombo, George Fisher, and Robert Welch. And it would be no exaggeration to state that this book might not have been possible without the interest and assistance of Joseph "Jakie" Hall.

The cheer and efficiency of Cecilia Forney, Julia Nardi, and Mary Sophia Smith are likewise greatly appreciated.

I am particularly grateful to Nancy Essig, Carol Ehrlich, and Chris Smith of the Johns Hopkins University Press for their diligent and imaginative work throughout.

Special thanks are in order to the Maryland State Arts Council, the Noxell Foundation, Robert and Jane Meyerhoff, Edwin A. Daniels, Jr., Leith and Benjamin H. Griswold III, Francis and Harriet Iglehart, and S. Bonsal White for their inestimable generosity and support.

Constantine Grimaldis lent his considerable energy, enthusiasm, and resources to this project, as did Fred Lazarus IV. My heartfelt thanks to both of them.

This book was heavily dependent upon the talent and cooperation of photographers Duane Suter and Chris Hartlove. I am also much obliged to Jim Burger for coming out of a richly deserved retirement and lending his remarkable photographic expertise.

I owe J. D. Considine and Scott Riddle a great debt for their helpful critical response and suggestions. As always, I've relied on the trusted counsel of Craig M. Gendler, Esquire.

And, of course, my toughest critics and staunchest defenders remain my wife, Esther Giller, and my son, Joe. They actually live with me by choice.

Finally, I want to thank my subject, Eugene Leake, for his patience, honesty, and good humor. A better man I've never known.

I shall never grow old while I have eyes to see with.
—Théodore Rousseau

For the ones who had a notion,
A notion deep inside,
That it ain't no sin to be glad you're alive.
—Bruce Springsteen

EUGENE LEAKE

The Maryland that Eugene Leake paints will be familiar to anyone who has driven north out of Baltimore for half an hour or so, past Loch Raven Reservoir to Jarrettsville Pike. The rolling green farmland and endless horse pastures, the densely wooded streams and four-corner towns compose the world this painter loves best. It is here, says Leake, that his two great passions—painting and nature—live on equal terms.

One can still find unspoiled forests and winding country lanes that would have enticed Théodore Rousseau or the young Claude Monet, two artists whom Leake greatly admires. Yet, things are changing in this region, and those changes have not escaped Leake's palette. "The choice of subject matter—why one chooses to paint a small town with a gas station, for instance—that may be sociological, I don't really know," Leake admits. "But for me, it says something about a part of Maryland that may be disappearing: the small rural towns. I like these farms out in the country with the silos that are now all white. The roofs are metal and they shine in the sun. And they're not gentleman farmer's farms. They're not like the big horse farms with the fancy white fences. They're not the moneymaking part of the world. They're the last of the small farmers."

Although a resident of the area for twenty-five years, Leake is not a native. Born August 31, 1911, in Jersey City, he lived as a youngster in New Jersey and New York. As is often the case, it takes an outsider to put a place in perspective: "When you think about a landscape painting, you also have to think that it's probably closer to another painting than it ever is to nature itself. Maybe I like this Maryland country so much because it reminds me at various times of Constable or Corot or Hopper. Whereas Maine, for example, doesn't. Maine makes me think of Marsden Hartley, Winslow Homer, Neil Welliver, and some other painters who've worked up there. But Maryland hasn't had that many distinguished painters. . . . There's a quietness and a gentleness to Maryland that is like the English landscape. It gets a little heavy here in the summer, with the yellow skies and the hot days. But we may be missing the boat by not painting more of that."

The second of three children, "Bud" Leake sensed early what he wanted to do in life and was fortunate enough to be born into a family that nurtured his artistic ambitions. He grew up in a house whose walls were hung with paintings collected by his maternal grandfather, Eugene Paige. In addition to canvases by such American painters as Ralph Blakelock and J. Francis Murphy, Leake recalls a painting by E. Irving Couse of "four Indians sitting around a camp-fire—I looked at it every night of my early life while I ate supper."

Around the age of eight, Leake's interest in painting, and landscape painting in particular, intensified. A family seam-stress who came to the house once a week gave him a copy of Alfred Sensier's monograph on the French Barbizon painter Jean-François Millet. Young Leake loved the book and read it again and again, poring over its black-and-white illustrations. At about the same time he began drawing in earnest. "I still have a pastel I did when I was eight years old that my uncle had framed. When you're a kid and your family frames one of your pictures, you think you're in the Metropolitan Museum of Art!" he laughs. "The funny thing is, it was a landscape. I think I did it from a photograph in the *National Geographic*. I didn't go through the stage a lot of kids do, drawing battleships and motorcycles. I was interested in something else."

Thus, Eugene Leake's twin passions of painting and nature grew steadily together. "We lived in a suburban area," he remembers. "A great influence was summer vacations, when I went way up in the woods of Maine with my father. Northern Maine was a tremendous influence—the romance of the dark pines and the water. Then we would spend one month at the shore. These were some of the first things I loved to paint.

"If you're an artist—no matter what age you are—there's an excitement you get from looking at paintings in museums. For me it ties in with my love of nature. Someone once wrote that almost all artists who keep at it, in a way, always paint their childhood. You never quite get over the marvelous mystery of being young and excited by those things in your childhood."

Leake continues: "And, in my case, I think love of landscape came also from love of landscape painting, per se. My family lived for a time in Montclair [New Jersey], which is where George Inness lived at the end of his life. Our house was on South Mountain Avenue, which was about a mile long. And at the other end of the street was the Montclair Art Museum, which had Innesses in its collection. I said to myself, this guy painted right around here. I thought that was terribly exciting and I liked his paintings, too."

As a teenager, Leake attended the Hill School in Potts-town, Pennsylvania. He did well in English and history, poorly in math and science. ("All I ever wanted to do was paint," he chuckles.) But the closest thing to an art class

Eugene Leake (right) *with brother, John, and their mother, Marion Paige Leake, at Cape Cod,*
ca. 1918

offered at the school was a manual training course. Leake managed to convince the headmaster to hire an art teacher. "Here was an artist who rode the train up from Philadelphia every Saturday morning to teach me and one other boy—two students out of 450," says Leake, his voice still tinged with disbelief. "This guy was so modern. The minute he got us started in painting, he said, 'Now look at all those marvelous colors out there. They have a purity and a luminosity. Don't screw them up!' I think back and I say, 'Who the hell *was* that guy? I can't remember his name. But he was talking like Josef Albers!' "

In 1930, Leake entered the Yale School of Fine Arts, at that time a classically structured, five-year baccalaureate program. Although he enjoyed the rigorous life drawing instruction and learned traditional underpainting techniques, Leake found the school's Beaux Arts orientation tedious and uninspiring. He left after four years.

Twenty-two and restless, Leake spent some time traveling through the Southwest. He journeyed to Mexico, where he saw the bold murals of Diego Rivera and Jose Orozco, and then on to California. At each stop along the way, he recorded his experiences in drawings and watercolors.

Returning to Connecticut, Leake built a small studio in Salisbury and set to work. He supported himself by paint-ing commissioned portraits and teaching some classes. An allowance from his father helped him through the leaner days. After studying for a time at the Art Students League, the young painter began taking his work around to New York galleries. Leake had his first one-man show at the Walker Gallery in 1937. The exhibition consisted primarily of expressionist watercolor landscapes, quite a few of which found buyers. Like many artists of his generation, Leake entered the juried exhibitions then frequently sponsored by major museums. As a result, his paintings were exhibited in national group shows at the Metropolitan Museum of Art, the Art Institute of Chicago, and the Brooklyn Museum. In 1939, he married Nora (Nonie) Bullitt of Louisville, Kentucky. ("The first year we were married, I think I earned $750. But it wasn't too bad. We had free rent in the studio and gin was a dollar a bottle!")

At the outbreak of World War II, Leake took a job in a defense plant. Soon thereafter, he joined the Navy, rising to the rank of lieutenant, and while in the service completed a number of watercolors. One summer, *Vanity Fair* editor Frank Crowninshield, a Bullitt family friend, happened to admire some of Leake's pictures. Crowninshield had the watercolors shipped to him in Southampton, Long Island, and put them on display. He sold nearly all of them.

Eugene Leake with his wife Nonie and daughters Nora (left) and Nina in Louisville, 1952
Photograph by James N. Keen

After the war, Leake found himself with a family to support (Nora had been born in 1942, Nina in 1944) and few prospects for employment. His wife and daughters had spent the war years with the Bullitts in Louisville, so it was there that Leake joined them. He worked briefly for a local radio station and then signed on to teach night classes in life drawing at the Art Center Association of Louisville. In 1949 he became its director.

Affiliated with the University of Louisville, the Art Center drew roughly a hundred students a year from the university, art schools, and the community at large. On its faculty was the German-born painter and intellectual Ulfert Wilkie, who counted Max Beckmann, Lyonel Feininger, Emil Nolde, and Ad Reinhardt among his artist friends, and who introduced Leake to sculptors David Smith and George Rickey.

Leake was an extremely capable administrator and enjoyed both directing and teaching at the Art Center. But painting remained his first love, and evenings, weekends, and summer vacations were devoted to the studio. One vacation during those years was especially memorable.

"In the summer of 1952 I was in Prout's Neck, Maine, and while there, I did some painting in a little barn with doors that opened out onto the grass, and beyond the grass, the rocks and the sea. At that time, I was continuing, particularly in watercolors, a series of very dark, horizontal, abstract landscapes. The last day there, which was a bright Maine day, I was inside the dark barn, doing dark watercolors, when I heard an old man with a scythe out in the sun. He stopped, wiped his brow, and asked if he could come in and cool off. I said, 'Certainly.'

"So he came in and said in his marvelous Maine accent, 'Whatcha doin'?'

'Well, I'm painting.'

'Kin I take a look?'

'Sure.'

"He came over, squinted his eyes, and said, 'Don't look like much ta me.' (And I don't think it was just the darkness of the painting and the barn, but the fact that it didn't look like much to him.) 'Tha *was* a painter fellow up here thet was pretty good.'

'Who was that?'

'Winslow Homer.'

'Come on, you're not old enough to have known him.'

'Hell I ain't,' he said.

"So he went on and told great stories about how his father, who was a fisherman, would keep some of Homer's paintings in his house during the winter; when Homer came back in the spring, he would go to the fisherman's house to pick up his painting and ask, 'How did you like the painting, being as you kept it all winter?' And usually the fisherman would say, 'Fine.' But one time he said, 'T'aint right.'

'Why?'

'Well, you've got the wind blowing one way and the waves goin' another. T'aint right!'

"So, after leaving Prout's Neck, and my talk with the old fisherman, I looked out the door of the barn, and I saw the bright, incredible light of summer, and when I went and looked at these dark paintings, I didn't think much of them, either. I can't say dramatically that this was the last time that I did an abstract painting, but it certainly got me thinking."

Spring Landscape, *1965*
Photograph by Jim Burger

After ten years as the Art Center's director, Leake felt as though he had reached a dead end. He was ready to change jobs and leave Louisville, but he knew that without a college degree (or two) significant advancement would be difficult. He decided to apply to Yale and complete the BFA requirements and while there earn a Master's degree as well. ("They accepted me, God knows why. Hell, I was twice as old as the other students.") In the fall of 1959, Eugene Leake, age forty-eight, went back to school.

The Yale School of Art and Architecture was a very different place from the staunchly conservative Yale School of Fine Arts Leake had left in boredom twenty-five years earlier. Josef Albers, the highly influential painter, designer, and Bauhaus esthetician, had just retired after eight years as chairman of the School of Art. He was responsible for Yale's mid-century prominence as a bastion of modernist theory and teaching in the arts. Albers had once summed up his philosophy about the essence and power of art in eight lines:

Josef Albers (lower right) *teaching a color class at Yale, 1952. Courtesy of The Josef Albers Foundation, Inc.*

The origin of art:
The discrepancy between physical fact and psychic effect
The content of art:
Visual formulation of our reaction to life
The measure of art:
The ratio of effort to effect
The aim of art:
Revelation and evocation of vision[1]

In spite of his recent retirement, the seventy-one-year-old Albers continued to make his presence felt. Leake reaped the benefits.

"I thought he was one of the greatest teachers anybody ever saw. He inspired in everybody a belief that art was important, not just games or personal expression; it really was something much bigger than you were. I was very lucky. Even though he was retired, he still came in almost every week.

---

1. Quoted in Eugen Gomringer's *Josef Albers* (New York: George Wittenborn, 1968), p. 7.

"Albers came to my studio one day," Leake recalls. "I was painting semi-abstract landscapes, horizontal bands of color. He said to me, 'I've heard about you. You are de old Prix de Rome—type painter. Mit underpainting und all dot garbage?' I said, 'Yeah, I learned all that.' And Albers looked at my painting and said, 'Vot you doing here? Dis is about color! It's a metamorphosis!'

"He had the most marvelous eye of any man I've ever seen. He'd point at your picture and say, don't look at it from the front all the time, come over here and look at it almost from the side. And he was right. The difference was amazing. Sometimes those horizontal bands changed so completely that you could see what was wrong with the painting—why it was inert, without a life of its own, where the problem was with the placement and the amount of color.

"Every once in a while he'd come to the Art Department and get the painting students together, maybe fifty in all. One time he began by saying, 'I see a lot of junk around here. Everybody is painting like New York City. Everybody wants to be De Kooning. If you're using a four-inch brush with all this elbow activity, get out a small brush and do the opposite. If you hate purple, use it. Do everything you hate instead of nursing yourself along in some awful way of trying to be something you're not.' He was terrific. I liked him a lot."

One of Albers's greatest legacies was hiring the best students to teach classes at Yale. Through this happy circumstance, Leake came to know the painters Bernard Chaet, William Bailey, and Neil Welliver, who remain his friends today.

Leake's plan for career advancement worked. Upon completion of his studies at Yale, job offers arrived from all over the country. "I said to Nonie, 'Well, where do you want to live?' And she said, 'Anywhere on the East Coast between Washington and Boston. I don't want to go to California or back to the South, and I don't want to live in the Midwest.' "

Among the art schools looking for leadership in the spring of 1961 was the Maryland Institute in Baltimore. The second-oldest art college in America (it had been incorporated in 1826 as the Maryland Institute for the Promotion of the Mechanic Arts), the once-grand institute had fallen on hard times. Following several decades of oppressive esthetic stagnation even more extreme than what Leake had encountered at Yale in the 1930s, the Maryland Institute had sought in 1957 to remedy its problems by hiring a "progressive" educator named Alfred P. Maurice as its di-

rector. One of Maurice's earliest (and most symbolic) acts in office was to throw the institute's collection of Elgin marble casts into the alley behind the school's Main Building. Within three years, Maurice was gone, full-time enrollment had plummeted to 270 (fewer than a dozen of these were painting majors), and morale could sink no lower.

Theodore ("Tubby") Sizer, one of Leake's art history professors at Yale, encouraged him to look into the president's job at the Maryland Institute. Sizer had lectured at the institute in the thirties before its decline and had been impressed with the school and the city of Baltimore. He saw great potential for both.

After visiting Baltimore and observing the institute, Leake agreed with Sizer. He became the president of the Maryland Institute School of Art in June 1961. His work was cut out for him.

Among the things the institute needed desperately were more students, new faculty, additional studio space, a better library, a bigger budget, and national accreditation. Leake began with new faculty. He brought painter-printmaker Peter Milton and sculptors Norman Carlberg and Stephanie Scuris from Yale and hired Albert ("Abby") Sangiamo, a Yale graduate who had taught at Morgan State College, to head the institute's Foundation Department.

Sangiamo recalls: "At his first meeting with the department chairmen, Bud said to them that he felt the institute couldn't become a good school again unless it had a strong fine arts program at its core. Now this is the school that had practically gotten rid of its painting major and was on its way to becoming an art education college. Bud made his intentions very clear."

Leake believed the reestablishment of the institute's reputation as a first-class painting school was the key to fulfilling its other needs. Thus, the overwhelming majority of his new faculty appointments were painters. Painting's long-lost status as a mandatory one-year course was restored; outstanding painters such as Fairfield Porter, Ad Reinhardt, Alex Katz, Jon Schueler, and Neil Welliver were brought in from New York and elsewhere as guest lecturers and critics. And Leake himself gave the school's self-esteem a major boost when one of his paintings, *Buoy No. 4*, was selected out of nearly ten thousand entries to be among seventy-four works in the Museum of Modern Art's "Recent Painting USA: The Figure" exhibition in 1962.

At about this time, Leake contacted Grace Hartigan, the nationally known abstract expressionist, who had moved to Baltimore from New York two years before. Hartigan accepted a position as director of the institute's fledgling graduate painting program, which in 1966 would become the Hoffberger School of Painting.

"Bud not only knew a lot about painting, he was passionately in love with the art of painting. He was extremely opinionated, but he didn't care if you argued with him. It

Buoy No. 4, *1962*

was fine with him. His point of view was his point of view, and he'd try to ram it down your throat. But then if you fought long enough, he was real nice about it," laughs Hartigan.

"To me, Bud was an 'expressionist' administrator, never afraid to take a chance or make a bold move," notes painter Raoul Middleman, whom Leake hired in his first year as president. "An incident typical of his 'expressionist' style occurred in the late sixties. I had suggested bringing a painter friend of mine, Paul Resika, down from New York as a guest lecturer. When Resika got here, he didn't want to lecture from slides. But his audience was too big to take to a museum. So Bud brought a museum to the institute. He hired a Pinkerton guard and had a truckload of paintings from the Lucas Collection, which was bequeathed to the institute and in storage at the Baltimore Museum of Art, driven to the school. It was incredible. Corot, Millet, Daubigny—all hanging in the B & O Station Building!"

Grace Hartigan describes another example of the Leake style: "In the late sixties, of course, there was a lot of student rebellion. At that time, the Hoffberger students had their studios in an awful building, which I believe was on Oliver Street. The windows were broken, the plumbing didn't work—it was pretty bad. So without my knowledge,

Eugene Leake, president, the Maryland Institute, College of Art, ca. 1962. Courtesy of the Maryland Institute, College of Art.
Photograph by Merle Edwards

my students drew up a list of complaints and they marched into Bud Leake's office. They said, 'If you don't meet our demands, we're going to take over your office.' Bud said, 'You want my office? You have it. Good-bye!' And he walked out, leaving them in his office!

"There was absolutely no red tape with Bud. If something was going wrong, I'd just call him up. I'd say, 'I've got too many students.' He'd say, 'Okay, we'll get another building.' "

By all accounts, Leake was a dynamic, supportive administrator, praised for his integrity and concern, an accessible leader who could make things happen through sheer energy and enthusiasm. Described by various faculty and staff members as an "amiable dictator" and a "benevolent autocrat," Leake made all the decisions and accepted full responsibility for them. As a painter himself, Leake took a genuine interest in the artists he hired, giving each of them complete freedom to teach in the manner he or she saw fit.

Leake's tireless and good-natured determination paid off. In his thirteen years as president, the Maryland Institute College of Art quadrupled its enrollment, tripled its faculty, and doubled its space through the acquisition of properties, including the Mount Royal Station. The library grew from 5,400 volumes to nearly 30,000, the budget increased ten-fold, and the school earned full national accreditation in 1967.

Despite an extremely demanding schedule, Leake never stopped painting. "I found that running the Maryland Institute interrupted my painting less than teaching," he remarks. "I've always said to young artists, don't overlook the possibility of being assistant dean at some art school. If you become a university dean, you're going to be on one committee after another, and they'll kill you. Your creative life will be gone—I'd rather be a broker. But if you go to a good art school where half the staff are artists anyway, you can probably survive. If you work forty hours a week, giving the guy what you owe him for the salary you're getting, then you've got a hell of a lot of time left to paint. So I did that for years and I think it interrupted my painting less than getting involved in a classroom would have."

Like any good painter, Leake's ideas about color and form were constantly growing, changing. In 1969, he traveled to Madrid and spent a week in the Prado Museum. There, a personal revolution that had begun seventeen summers before in Prout's Neck, Maine, was completed. Leake explains it this way: "For my part, it was a revolt against modern painting. If I had to see another painting that was pure red, blue, orange. . . . All the abstract painters and

Eugene Leake, 1971. Courtesy of the Maryland Institute, College of Art.
Photograph by Joan C. Netherwood

most of the expressionists were using bright, powerful, 'French' colors, high in key. And people would buy them because they love color. You can sell color anywhere. Tintoretto once said, 'Give me the drama of black and white at high noon and I'll give you a great painting. I can buy colors on the Rialto!' Inwardly, I was rebelling against the colors of one hundred years of French painting, from Manet on.

"So when I went to the Prado, I got so excited by the dark mystery of Goya and his powerful relationship to the world around him—the great drawings, the Disasters of War, the 'Caprichos'—I just couldn't believe it. And I found his portraits among the greatest in the world.

"Then I stepped into that room of Velazquez and it didn't look like the kind of color you see on the screen in an art history class. It just breathed—that sky behind *The Surrender of Breda*, the space in that marvelous landscape, the battle in the distance, the men and the horses. And those grays and halftones, Jesus! For me, it really was a revolt against one kind of color in favor of another.

"I walked out of that museum and I said, I'm never going to paint any abstract or semi-abstract pictures again as long as I live. So having always loved landscapes, I came back and got the French easel and I started to do what I hadn't done in a long time: go outdoors and paint landscape. And I've been doing it ever since."

Not surprisingly, Leake's esthetic awakening was accompanied by a change in technique. "When I came home from the Prado, with my interest with grays, I went back to the earth palette that I'd learned at Yale in the 1930s. That's a great traditional palette: terre vert green, yellow ochre, ultramarine blue. And all the reds are earth reds: Mars red, Venetian red, Indian red, burnt siena. To that I'd add Prussian blue or a black and then I got enamored of some of the marvelous greens, like oxide of chromium. But I now make greens out of blue and yellow, rather than buying them in the tube, because I can mix a little red with it quickly and kill anything that's too harsh and get exactly the green I want.

"Technique, to me, is always changing a little bit. I don't have one that I learned once and use forever and for always. It grows, I hope. Lately, I've been painting sunrises and I've gone back to the primary palette: cadmium yellow, cadmium red, alizarin crimson, ultramarine blue. I can mix everything out of those colors. You might add black to that, and that's all you need. So let's say five or six colors. I've never seen a painting yet I couldn't do with five or six colors.

"I think that colors become fresher, too, if you don't have a formula. Albers was a great influence here, also. He just had a horror of all these books on color theory. He said, throw it all out; it's all visual. The only way to find out about color is to see it and compare one with another. That's what his whole technique was about.

"I did learn to underpaint and occasionally I put a warm-ish, toned ground on the whole canvas, the way Titian and Goya and Constable did, and then instead of glazing over it, I paint directly over it. I'll leave some of the canvas showing through, and it does marvelous things in terms of unifying the picture. And sometimes I work on an absolutely pure white canvas. I don't have any rule about it.

"I've done fairly large paintings in one sitting that hold up without going back at all. Then I've done pictures where I've gone back four or five times for a couple of hours each. Ten, eleven, twelve hours is usually enough. My temperament is such that if I start to get too many details I get picky and I don't like what I see. It destroys my space and color and everything else."

Upon his return from Spain, Leake chose for subject matter the countryside surrounding his Garrison, Maryland, home. (The Leakes had rented this 1690 farmhouse—one of the oldest standing in Baltimore County—after living for a year in northern Baltimore City). When the house was put up for sale in 1973, Leake and his wife moved to another charming old farmhouse in Monkton, just west of the Baltimore County–Harford County line. Leake wasted no time converting the barn into a studio and picked up where he left off, painting the rural landscape of Maryland.

Eugene Leake in the Garrison studio, 1972.
Photograph by William Klender

The paintings done in the years following the move to Monkton are, quite simply, Leake's best work. They belong to a tradition that can be traced back to the Barbizon and early Impressionist schools, yet reflect a sensibility firmly rooted and cultivated in twentieth-century America. Leake has never been a careerist, choosing instead to live an independent, even isolated, existence far from the clamor of the New York art world. His work, if not as well known as that of his peers, is every bit as strong. Several of the paintings reproduced in this book have hung in group exhibitions alongside canvases by Leake's most respected contemporaries. Tougher than the works of Fairfield Porter, gentler than those of Neil Welliver, the landscapes of Eugene Leake are as honest and forceful as the man himself.

"When I first met Bud, he was painting in more of a West Coast, Richard Diebenkorn–kind of style," recalls Grace Hartigan. "And I think he found his own way in the years since then. It's an interesting thing, and I'm not quite sure how to express it. Bud really feels that his way is the way to paint. And he makes it very clear that he thinks that's the way everybody should, except that he doesn't get mad at you if you don't. That's a rare quality; he doesn't cut people off from himself.

"As Bud has gotten older, he's become more and more deeply passionate about other art, art of the past. He feels a solidarity with tradition, almost like a colleague. And he reads artists' words almost as though they were conversations with him. I find that fascinating.

"Bud has a very wise understanding of where his work is in relationship to the world, a mature look at the whole picture. And I think that is an admirable attitude on his part. I find it extremely difficult with artists where the ambition for the work is all out of whack with the content and the nature of the work itself. Bud has never had that problem. He knows exactly what he's doing."

Leake felt the urge to paint more strongly than ever, while his patience for running an increasingly bureaucratic Maryland Institute was wearing thin. He announced his retirement, effective June 1974. "After the place grew up and got more committees and became more like a college and less like an open, free art school, I began to get awfully restless. I thought to myself, why don't I just quit? It was a gamble. We didn't have that much money then, but figured we wouldn't starve. So I resigned at age sixty-two. And I must say everyone at the Maryland Institute was terribly nice about it, and very generous, too."

Having left the institute, Leake found he missed the regular contact with students. In the fall of 1974, he became the Johns Hopkins University's first artist-in-residence, a position he still holds today.

The last few years have seen bittersweet times for Leake. His beloved wife, Nonie, died of cancer in 1980, and his own arthritis necessitated a pair of total hip replacements two years later. However, his recovery was speedy and complete, allowing him to get back to work virtually upon release from the hospital. Leake's days brightened considerably when he married Victoria S. Costello in the summer of 1983.

And through it all has been painting, the demanding and magical endeavor that Leake loves so dearly, yet claims to understand so little. "It's a very mysterious process," he says. "I think every painting has a life of its own, in addition to the life it has as an expression of real space or figures or anything else. There's a balance somewhere between what you decide to put into a painting and what you leave out. But, you know, two days in a row I won't feel exactly the same about it. It's like Hokusai, the great Japanese painter and printmaker. When he was 75, he said, 'Don't look at anything I did before I was 65.' And he meant it. He said, 'I'm going to live a long time. I'm 75 now, wait

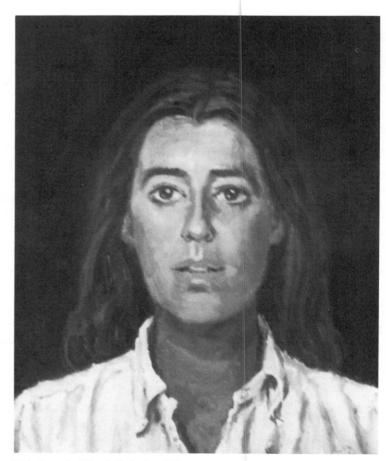

Vicky (portrait of Victoria S. Leake, 1984).

till you see what I do when I'm 90—it'll begin to get good. By the time I'm 105, I might really know what I'm doing.' That's the way I think painting is."

A smile creases his tanned, leathery face as he says this. Then, the clear blue eyes turn serious for a moment. "I just feel that the paintings that work right are the ones where I've found the truth of a given hour."

Eugene Leake, 1986
Photograph by Jim Burger

PLATES

1 Pocock Meadow—June. 1984

"This is farmland. There are often horses grazing in the pastures. The Little Gunpowder Falls, which forms the foreground, is shallow but moving and has trout in it farther up the meadow to the north.

"As Paul Weiss, the philosopher at Yale, said, if you go from wild landscape and you creep back toward the urban world, you get to this intermediate zone that is rural farmland. And we feel comfortable in this rural space—a landscape that has been touched by the hand of man. So that's where we are in this painting. The land is typically open. There's a classic quality that makes me think of Poussin or Claude and sometimes Constable. It is English and French, and yet it's very American. And the American quality, I think, comes from a certain clarity of light.

"I fluctuate a bit between the need to be quite specific as to what kind of tree that is, and other times more generalized. I think that's due to the fact that your per-ceptions and feelings as an individual change almost week by week. Anyway, this painting is a June day, so clear and so marvelous that you wish it would last forever. The grass is no longer the bright green you see in April or early May. It's already been mowed once, so it has a sort of tawny look. I'm interested above all else in the color that's really there. Not in the emotional input of making it brilliant green because it'll make a more interesting painting, but in getting it exactly as it looked that morning. I must have painted that place, almost the same spot, at least ten or fifteen times, and every time it is different. I suppose, in a way, the place has a natural order. I worked on this painting for three mornings. And never more than an hour and a half or two hours each because the light changes so dramatically. So I'd go down the same hour each morning. Fortunately, I had three good days in a row, when the light was almost exactly the same."

2 Landscape with White Dog. 1983

"I think this landscape, painted at My Lady's Manor, is very typical of parts of Maryland. It has the smokiness of late summer and the quiet sense of distance enhanced by the haze.

"I painted this picture on a very hot, slightly misty August day. The grass is already getting to be an orange sort of color. A white dog moved across that little path and I just stuck him in there. The painting's really not about him. Most of the time, there are no people, no tractors in my landscapes. And it's because most of the time they aren't there. If I'm painting at a spot for two or three hours, and a guy walks across the scene for five or ten seconds, well, he isn't really part of that thing to me. It seems forced to put him in.

"Sometimes when the sky appears flat, I mix a large batch of the right color and put it on fairly thickly. Opaque paint expresses the light of a sky better than thin washes or glazes. As in this painting, the color of the sky sets the light and tone for the whole scene."

**3 August Sunrise I.
1985**

"In the summer of '85 I did a number of sunrises from the fence line looking east on our own little farm. The view is endlessly varied and evocative. Sometimes I get a good painting of this hour. I get set up the evening before so that everything is ready to go the minute the light is right. This picture is 12" x 16" and was done in a half-hour, but only after a few unsuccessful tries on other mornings. The color of the foreground field and the trees, bushes, and fields in the middle distance is, for me, the picture's great mystery and its gamble, as well.

"I should add that just before doing this painting I had been looking at some of Titian's late works. The backgrounds for some of his figure compositions are, in my opinion, the essence of atmospheric painterliness—they explode with expressive color and great freedom. You can see this, for example, in the mountains, sea, and sky of The Rape of Europa *at the Gardner Museum in Boston."*

**4 August Sunrise II.
1985**

"The small picture, August Sunrise I, *seemed to hold up after having it around for a few weeks, so I decided to paint a seven-foot sunrise. I tied the stretcher to a tree and leaned it up against the fence. The day before, I had put a tone over the whole surface so there wouldn't be so much white canvas to battle, but even at that I had to go out three mornings in a row to get it done. Fortunately, I was blessed with three very similar skies, so it took only a bit of invention on my part. This is the same spot, incidentally, from which I later painted* September Pasture with a Horse.*"*

5 Evening Tree. 1980

"I live in Harford County, on the eastern edge of a tract of land (deeded in 1716) known as My Lady's Manor. There were never any grand estates in this lovely, rolling area. It always had fairly small farms and simple farmhouses.

"This tree is on the east corner of my farm. Pocock Road is just behind me, and the studio-barn is hidden in the middle distance. In the mysterious light of early evening, what is a rather unspectacular scene by day evokes another kind of poetry.

"When tackling a sunset or even the gentle, early evening light, you have to work intuitively and spontaneously—almost unconsciously. This painting seems to have a suppressed romanticism and fluidity that express some of the moving quality of evening as the tree rises in darkness against the sky. It was painted with a primary palette: ultramarine blue, prussian blue, alizarin crimson, chrome yellow, and cadmium red."

6 Pocock Meadow with December Sky. 1981

"Looking north from the Little Gunpowder bridge at the bottom of Pocock Road, you'll see a flat meadow with distant trees which lends itself to the classic low-horizon landscape. Sometimes you get these spectacular cerulean blue skies and warm violet clouds overhead. The meadow's early winter grass appears warm, too, in the sunlight. There are often cattle grazing on this land, but not this day."

7 Winter Horses. 1983

"I've painted this a hundred times, too. It was done looking out the studio window. Again, this is rural land where there are open fields and patches of woods. If you keep going through those woods on the left, you come to where March Wood and Stream—Hutchins Mill was made. It's all part of the same woods.

"One winter morning, I went to the studio and there I saw this incredible sky and the dark horses against the snow. I'm lucky to have a few horses board on my farm. They keep showing up in the land-scape—more as spots of color than descriptions of thoroughbreds, however.

"I moved the horizon way down because I thought the sky that morning was the key to the whole thing. That's a device as old as the seventeenth century or before. But if you worried about it, you'd never do anything. You'd say, 'God, what am I doing? Is this seventeenth century? Eighteenth century? Nineteenth century?' Maybe the greatest landscapes were painted in the nineteenth century and what I'm doing now may be an apocryphal append-age. But I'm not going to worry about it. I've got to do it because I love it. Wasn't it Delacroix who said that the artist when he gets too intellectual gets lost, and the only way out is to return to nature?"

8 September Pasture with a Horse. 1985

"After finishing the big sunrise painting (August Sunrise II), I was out one morning about two hours past sunrise and saw an incredibly warm, brownish cloud formation against a brilliant blue sky. I was galvanized into another painting right then. That morning the sun broke through in spots causing the green in the foreground to glow with light; the 'red' horse was there, too.

"The old trees and scrub growth in the middle distance were once clear meadow with a small stream. It is now a swamp with (I am told) an endangered species of turtle to be found on occasion. To me, the swamp makes for better painting than the well-groomed meadow of ten years ago. The colors and forms are diverse and exciting."

9 Fence Line.
1977

"This section of the board fence on my farm is close to the dark rocks near the place where the fox hunters jumped (see March Rocks, Trees, and White Sky). Fence Line *was painted on a spring morning with the fresh greens so beautiful against a clear blue June sky. The fence itself weaves in and out as the violet shadows of* the white boards interrupt the long, diagonal lines. Fences are characteristic of horse farm country, and maybe this one is also somehow symbolic of the break between wild nature and the infringing farmlands or even the encroachment of creeping suburbia."

10 March Wood and Stream—Hutchins Mill. 1981

"This was painted only a few hundred yards from Pocock Meadow—June. But it's a different time of year, a different time of day. The terrain isn't wild, it's woodland that goes with the farm. Cattle graze under the trees in the summer. There might be fifty acres of woods like this. Strangely enough, that stream is almost gone now. It's overgrown with weeds, and you can't see the water any more.

'I found that what excited me there was that it was March—very early spring—when the light is soft, just beginning to sparkle, and there's no green as yet. And I hope that here, too, I captured the colors that are really there. I didn't try to emotionalize them or to use them for esthetic organization or anything like that. I don't think any two of these trees are exactly the same color. That is the way it was; it isn't like a formula. And the painting does seem to have some space. Not just as you move into it through perspective, but through light and color.

"In order to work on this fairly large canvas, I braced it against a tree near a bridge that crosses the stream. As with Pocock Meadow—June, I worked on the painting for three mornings."

11 Black Winter Stream. 1984

"I have returned time and again to paint this intimate place, a quiet bend in a small stream with three trees on the bank and the woods beyond. This particular canvas was painted in December and is typical of a dark day on the edge of the woods. One could keep moving around this site in a tight circle and come up with a cycle of new paintings which would emphasize the different lights, seasons, and moods of a secret place. Summer Stream, *for instance, was also painted here.*

"In the Guggenheim Museum catalogue for the exhibition 'New Horizons in American Art' (1985), Lisa Dennison talks about the approach to landscape painting in the nineteenth century: 'Through a portrayal of the vastness and grandeur, the isolated, moody and often lonely aspects of nature, landscape painting addressed spiritual ideas.' Perhaps some of this attitude still persists."

12 March Rocks, Trees, and White Sky. 1983

"This is the same place on my farm where I painted Black Rocks—*that was summer, this is March. The whole area can't be more than a hundred yards across and two hundred deep. It's surrounded by a fence to keep the horses out, since the ground is full of rocks and old foxholes plus a healthy crop of wild cherry, which is poisonous for horses.*

"The painting came easily. I mixed large batches of the big color areas and painted wet-in-wet, using a very simplified palette of Indian red, Venetian red, ultramarine blue and yellow ochre. The color on the ground suggests old, wet leaves, and the cast shadows were some sort of cool violet-grey.

"I would like to paint this spot someday in the rain because weather changes always make new paintings, and many of my paintings, I've found, are about weather."

13 Black Rocks. 1979

"Near the barn on my farm is an outcropping of dark rocks in a thicket of wild cherry trees, blackberry bushes, honeysuckle, and poison ivy. It was Courbet's painting that inspired me to look closely at nearby rocks and trees. In certain lights, this unseemly spot takes on a majestic quality due to the way the light hits the biggest of the trees and filters through the leaves. Black Rocks *was painted in June.*

"I don't think about such things when I'm painting, but it occurs to me that we have become accustomed in the twentieth century to emphasize form over content, and that may not be such a hot idea after all. For instance, around the turn of the century, Gustav Mahler said, 'The ever new and changing content determines the form.' I like to think this painting works the same way."

**14 Deer Creek, Dark Day.
1981–82**

"Another place I've painted a hundred times. This is Deer Creek at the bottom of Telegraph Hill, about nine miles from my house.

"The only people I run into there are fishermen. For the most part, people are very nice. Usually, they look and you can see right away they're kind of disappointed. Occasionally, someone will hang around and chat and I'll say, 'You know, if you saw Johnny Unitas playing football and you went out on the field while he was in the pocket and started to talk to him, I think he'd say, "I've lost my concentration."' It may not look it, but to paint you've got to concentrate.' And the guy will say, 'Oh, I'm sorry.' And that's that. Sometimes when I'm painting

I don't even know where I am, and sometimes I feel as if my brush was touching things I see in the landscape rather than the canvas.

"I started this painting on a clear day but didn't like what I came up with. So I rubbed it out, put on a priming color, and came back on a beautiful, dark summer day. This time I was able to pull it all together in a few hours. The colors on gray days have a rich intensity. The water, for example, is a particularly mysterious color. It isn't green and it isn't quite brown. I'm not sure exactly how to describe it, but I know that if you get the color right, you capture the deep silence of that stream."

**15 Summer Stream.
1979**

"The Little Gunpowder Falls cuts across Houck's Mill Road about a mile above Pocock Road. I'd crossed the bridge here on walks in the area and was always attracted by the water just south of the bridge as it moved rapidly over a rocky section by a bank overhung with trees. In summer the shallow water and bright sun-light turned the stream bed an earth red, which the varied greens complemented so naturally. It was an intimate spot of no dramatic consequence; one could easily pass it by. Yet, it expressed to me so much of what I've come to feel and enjoy about summer."

**16 Summer Bridge.
1985**

"This bridge is no soaring span across sparkling waters, but a very ordinary little bridge with bending guard rails, half-covered with weeds. Late in the afternoon the trees were dark against the light sky, and the whole thing seemed broodingly hot and mysterious. I was interested here in the contrast between light and dark—in the weight and tension that result from such contrast.

"Clyfford Still once said to me, 'I have never painted a white painting—white is too cruel. My blacks are warm and human.' "

17 Pocock Road—October. 1981

"I walk here with my dogs so often that people in passing cars have dubbed me the 'menace of Pocock Road.' (Fortunately, since there's only one farm on a mile-long stretch of Pocock, there's not much traffic.) This spot is just a few hundred yards up the hill from the bridge over the Little Gunpowder Falls.

"One October afternoon the simplified forms and colors you so often find when you're looking into the sun suggested a painting immediately. Ruskin once noted that grass under these conditions isn't green but a strange gray-orange—or so it seems."

18 North of Shawsville. 1981

"The road from which I painted this low horizon farmland is actually more east of Shawsville than north, but I titled the painting before I checked the map. Since I am neither a chronicler nor a keeper of records, I never bothered to change it.

"I've always been excited by the sense of vast space and poetry this place suggests. I've painted it in different lights and at various times of the year. This picture was done on a bright June day. The foreground field is fresh and unmowed, and the sky is clear. Nothing stays the same for long, however. Even though North of Shawsville *was painted in the last five years, the view has already changed considerably."*

**19 Cows in the Snow.
1985**

*"On Bradenbaugh Lane there is a small
dairy farm where I found a convenient
place to sketch cows. One February day I
made this small painting of the herd hud-
dled together in the snow near a feeder.
The day was very gray and in the sky
were horizontal bands of clouds which
complemented the dark, horizontal marks
of the cows. I did another painting,*
Cows in the Rain, *from the same spot
and later a summer cow scene.*

*"In 1909 Monet said: 'As long as
constant commerce with the outside world
can maintain the ardor of my curiosity,
and my hand remains the prompt and
faithful servant of my perception, I have
nothing to fear from old age. I have no
other wish than a close fusion with
nature.'"*

**20 Winter Farm with
a Stream.
1985**

"I almost never seem to get what I want in a painting unless I keep going back to the same place over and over again, and so it was with the site. Perhaps this painting was subconsciously inspired by Monet's Vineyards in the Snow *(1873, Virginia Museum of Fine Arts, Richmond).*

"This is a dairy farm in Harford County which borders on Route 165, St. Clair Bridge Road and Deer Creek. It was a warmish, early March day, but more snow was on the way and the temperature dropped about ten degrees while I was painting. A farmer in a pickup truck stopped to see what was going on. After watching for a while, he asked if he had time to go up the hill to get his friend who owned the farm so that he could watch his land get born again—that's the way he put it."

21 Storm over Dairy Farm. 1985

"The way this farm on the Old York Road (I believe it's called 'Manor Farm') sits on a slight rise of otherwise flat land has often attracted me. I also like the mass of small buildings, barns, and silos. I started this painting in April of 1985 but never really liked it. However, the following July or early August we had a rash of violent thunderstorms with marvelous dark skies. Just before one of these storms broke I raced out to the site and, having reprimed the canvas with a middle grey tone, set to work in a feverish flurry of brush-dropping energy to try and capture the light on the roofs, the stormy sky, and the dark mood."

22 Farm and Pond. 1984

"Sometimes I just drive around looking for sites that interest me, for whatever reason. But I can be fooled because what looks exciting in one light can be a complete dud in another. The magic will be gone.

"One October day I spotted this farm with a pond on Carea Road. The place had a clear white-and-green structure that appealed to me. The light was behind the barns, and the shadows on the buildings were cool and bluish. I did a number of sketches and then went back after a few weeks, but everything was wrong. A year later I returned on another clear October morning and there it was as I first saw it: ready to paint."

23 Norrisville Houses. 1985

"Norrisville is a quiet rural spot on Route 23 in Harford County. It must have been founded just before the Civil War. The village, with a population of about a hundred, has one garage, a logging business, a small, boarded-up store, and many white houses. Behind the garage rests an old shed that was once a blacksmith's shop, an abandoned school bus, and then woods. Some of the houses need paint; rusting cars hide in the weeds. Farmland creeps right up to the highway, and cows are never far away.

"I painted this picture along the roadside on a partly cloudy day in November. What comes across, I think, is not the forlorn aspect of Norrisville, but rather the look of typical early twentieth-century houses in a small Maryland town."

24 Troyer Road—July. 1983

"There are a couple of well-run farms on Troyer Road, just a mile from Route 23. This one has several old barns, grain bins (dryers), and a shiny new barn. I did this painting in the morning on a warm July day. The corn already had a reddish look in certain lights, and I liked the single pole, which helped define the space, the guard rail, and the blue shadow on the grey road.

"I have talked to the man who owns this place. He is young and already farms other big fields across the road. Some people say that small farms can't make it any longer, but you wouldn't know it if you roam the back roads of this part of the country. These small farms stretch all the way to outer Philadelphia and west to the Appalachians.

"Looking at this picture reminds me of something Albers once said to me: 'If you read poetry into my painting, okay. But I didn't put it there.'

"I like to put it there when I can."

25 Susquehanna Boat Yard and Bridge. 1985

"My country meanderings have often taken me to Havre de Grace looking for expanses of water. The river and its bridges are marvelous to paint. I seem to go there more often in the winter than during the white sail and blue sky time of year. This sketch was done from the Perryville side of the river looking south to Havre de Grace. The junk-filled end of a boat yard looked good for painting—the kind of place that has more than smooth grass and white boats. The river was high this day and the water muddy. The grays and whites and browns had a fine unity: an envelope. It was quiet and perhaps forlorn.

"Behind the apparent ease of such painting there is a darker side. Monet wrote to a friend in 1890: 'I am in a black mood and profoundly disgusted with my painting. It is a continual torture—It is enough to drive one raving mad to try to render the weather, the atmosphere, the ambience.' How often I've felt this way myself."

**26 Corner on Route 23
North.
1985**

"Sometimes good paintings can be made from unlikely subjects such as this helter-skelter corner with its store, signs, parked cars, tilted poles, and sheds. Everything here seems to have fallen into place by chance, and one has the feeling that the whole thing could revert to a corn field be-fore long. It suggests to me a perilous balance between commerce and farm. This little intersection would be dull indeed without the many colored signs, which may have been what first lured me to paint this site."

**27 Smith Hardware.
1985**

*"Like other small towns I paint, Jarretts-
ville has a very rural American look that
I like. It remains untouched by the hands
of city planners who would probably do
something sensible with its pragmatic,
natural growth. But then it wouldn't be
as good to paint—at least not for me.*

*"I also like this hardware store, inside
and out. I find it very country and very*
*appealing. But all of this is kind of liter-
ary; and as a painter, it is what I see
that carries the weight. Perhaps here the
attraction was the way the road bends
into the central part of the painting, the
poles, the odd color of the buildings, and
the dark notes of the cars which give the
picture scale and a definition of space."*

**28 Shawsville.
1975**

"On the road to Norrisville, a few miles north of Madonna, there are a few houses, a family-type gas station, some barns, a silo, and the Southern States store that together make up the town called Shawsville. It is just a bend in the road away from the junction of Route 439. Shawsville has appealed to me as a great place to make a small-town-on-the-highway painting because of the way the road curves into the middle distance. The white house with its gas pump, the highway sign, the overhanging trees, and the spattering of sheds that lead up the gentle hill to the barn and silo—I have painted this spot a lot over the past twelve years. The gas pump disappeared several years after this painting was made, but the rest is still the same, and nowadays I see a few horses grazing in the small pasture on the left."

29 Madonna Winter. 1979

"There's Madonna, a classic rural Maryland village. It's typical also of small American crossroads anywhere. It has a branch bank, an auto repair shop, a country store with one gas pump, a state fire tower, a large church down the road, and a sprinkling of houses spreading out into the country.

"I like painting outdoors in the winter. Winter has a clarity and light of its own. If it's 32 degrees or above, I can paint all right. If it's 22, that's another story. I wear heavy, lined boots and warm gloves. I paint without a glove on my right hand for a while, then stop and warm it up. Painting outdoors the way I do, I couldn't live in Connecticut, for example. I'd be studio-bound all winter. Here, I can get out 80 to 90 percent of the time. You look at the average temperatures in Maryland, it'll be 38 during January. Well, that means some days are up to 40, 42.

"I think this painting works pretty well. There's a little white car over on the right parked in front of the building that sells gas from one pump. You've got the typical green road signs, the mailbox—it's unromanticized and unsentimentalized."

**30 Hunters Mill.
1984**

"At Argenteuil, a suburb of Paris, Monet painted trains, rivers, streets, factories, bridges, snow, woods, farms, horses, cows, and fields. My selection of subject matter in this part of the world is no different.

"This is a now-defunct paper mill out in northern Baltimore County. There are a couple of houses nearby, but it's an almost forgotten, semi-industrial site. I've done quite a few paintings of this spot. But I'm not interested in a closed factory the way a sociologist or a documentary photographer would be. What interested me, I guess, was the light of early spring, the space, the shadows, the variety of greens, and, of course, that smokestack. Maybe I like those buildings because the architecture gives a kind of geometry of structure to the painting that allows these generalized areas of foliage to move into space.

"When you first look at the picture, you see this clump of weeds on the right. Then your eye goes to the road sign. Then it moves up and around to the trees on the right which lead to the stack. You come down from there and to the left, and you're on the road, as though you were walking or driving."

List of Plates

1
Pocock Meadow—June
1984
Oil on canvas
42″ × 50″
Collection of Mr. and Mrs. John
Brentnall Powell, Jr.

2
Landscape with White Dog
1983
Oil on cancas
42″ × 60″
Collection of the artist. Courtesy of
C. Grimaldis Gallery.

3
August Sunrise I
1985
Oil on canvas board
12″ × 16″
Collection of the artist. Courtesy of
C. Grimaldis Gallery.

4
August Sunrise II
1985
Oil on canvas
72″ × 84″
Collection of the artist. Courtesy of
C. Grimaldis Gallery.

5
Evening Tree
1980
Oil on canvas
48″ × 66″
Courtesy of Mercantile–Safe Deposit
& Trust Company.

6
Pocock Meadow with December Sky
1981
Oil on canvas
18″ × 24″
Private collection.

7
Winter Horses
1983
Oil on canvas
42″ × 42″
Collection of Mr. and Mrs. Richard Blue, Jr.

8
September Pasture with a Horse
1985
Oil on canvas
60″ × 75″
Collection of the artist. Courtesy of
C. Grimaldis Gallery.

9
Fence Line
1977
Oil on canvas
48″ × 48″
Collection of the artist. Courtesy of
C. Grimaldis Gallery.

10
March Wood and Stream—Hutchins Mill
1981
Oil on canvas
60″ × 75″
Washington County Museum of Fine Arts,
Hagerstown, Maryland.

11
Black Winter Stream
1984
Oil on canvas
48″ × 66″
Courtesy of C. Grimaldis Gallery.

12
March Rocks, Trees, and White Sky
1983
Oil on canvas
48″ × 66″
Private collection.

13
Black Rocks
1979
Oil on canvas
60″ × 75″
Collection of Mr. and Mrs. George L.
Bunting, Jr.

14
Deer Creek, Dark Day
1981–82
Oil on canvas
48″ × 66″
Courtesy of Noxell Corporation.

15
Summer Stream
1979
Oil on canvas
42″ × 42″
Courtesy of Summit & Elizabeth
Trust Company.

16
Summer Bridge
1985
Oil on canvas
42″ × 48″
Courtesy of C. Grimaldis Gallery.

17
Pocock Road—October
1981
Oil on canvas
16″ × 20″
Collection of the artist. Courtesy of
C. Grimaldis Gallery.

18
North of Shawsville
1981
Oil on canvas
60″ × 79″
Owensboro Museum of Fine Art,
Owensboro, Kentucky.

19
Cows in the Snow
1985
Oil on canvas
12″ × 16″
Collection of the artist. Courtesy of
C. Grimaldis Gallery.

20
Winter Farm with a Stream
1985
Oil on canvas
36″ × 48″
Collection of the artist. Courtesy of
C. Grimaldis Gallery.

21
Storm over Dairy Farm
1985
Oil on canvas
36″ × 48″
Collection of the artist. Courtesy of
C. Grimaldis Gallery.

22
Farm and Pond
1984
Oil on canvas
48″ × 60″
Courtesy of C. Grimaldis Gallery.

23
Norrisville Houses
1985
Oil on canvas
42″ × 54″
Collection of the artist. Courtesy of
C. Grimaldis Gallery.

24
Troyer Road—July
1983
Oil on canvas
30″ × 36″
Courtesy of Mr. and Mrs. Francis N.
Iglehart.

25
Susquehanna Boat Yard and Bridge
1985
Oil on paper
24″ × 30″
Courtesy of C. Grimaldis Gallery.

26
Corner on Route 23 North
1985
Oil on canvas
24″ × 30″
Collection of the artist. Courtesy of
C. Grimaldis Gallery.

27
Smith Hardware
1985
Oil on canvas
16″ × 14″
Collection of the artist. Courtesy of
C. Grimaldis Gallery.

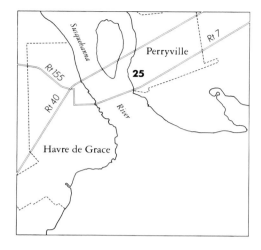

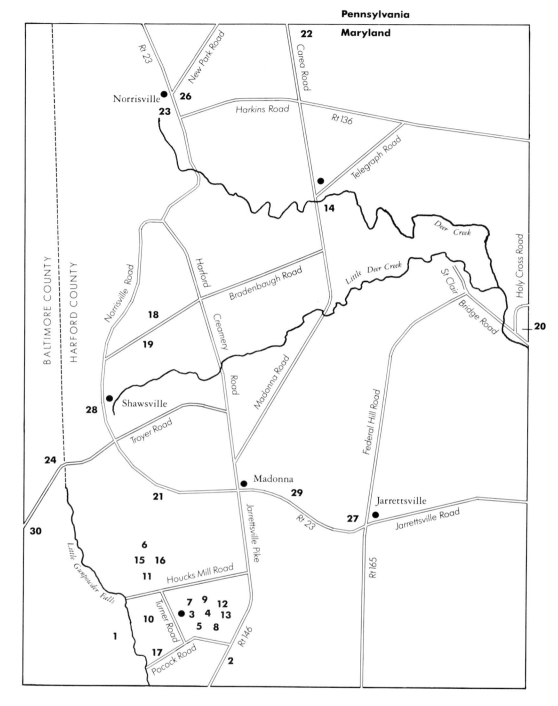

28
Shawsville
1975
Oil on canvas
36″ × 42″
Courtesy of Piper & Marbury.

29
Madonna Winter
1979
Oil on canvas
18″ × 24″
Collection of the artist. Courtesy of
C. Grimaldis Gallery.

30
Hunters Mill
1984
Oil on canvas
24″ × 22″
Collection of Mr. and Mrs. G. Cheston
Carey, Jr.

All color transparencies except numbers 10,
15, and 18 were taken by Duane Suter.

Selected One-Man Exhibitions

C. Grimaldis Gallery, Baltimore
Green Mountain Gallery, New York
Hamilton Gallery, Charleston, South Carolina
Jacobs Ladder Gallery, Washington, D.C.
Johns Hopkins University, Baltimore
Maryland Institute, College of Art, Baltimore
National Academy of Sciences, Washington, D.C.
Tatistcheff and Company, New York
Towson State University, Baltimore
University of Louisville, Louisville, Kentucky
University of Kentucky, Lexington
Walker Gallery, New York
York College, York, Pennsylvania

Selected Group Exhibitions

Art Institute of Chicago
Art Museum of South Texas, Corpus Christi
Baltimore Museum of Art

Brooklyn Museum of Art
Butler Institute of American Art, Youngstown, Ohio
Cincinnati Museum of Art
Guild Hall Museum, East Hampton, New York
Hirschl and Adler Galleries, New York
Jersey City Museum, Jersey City, New Jersey
M. Knoedler and Company, New York
Metropolitan Museum of Art, New York
Museum of Modern Art, New York
Owensboro Museum of Fine Art, Owensboro, Kentucky
Betty Parsons Gallery, New York
Pennsylvania Academy of the Fine Arts, Philadelphia
Philadelphia Museum of Art

Public Collections

Baltimore Museum of Art
Corcoran Gallery of Art, Washington, D.C.
Owensboro Museum of Fine Art, Owensboro, Kentucky
J. B. Speed Art Museum, Louisville, Kentucky
University of Louisville, Louisville, Kentucky
University of North Carolina, Greensboro
Washington County Museum of Fine Arts, Hagerstown, Maryland